IMAGES OF
CHESTER

Photographed by John Curtis

SALMON

INTRODUCTION

Few cities in England have such a wealth of historic buildings as Chester, the beautiful county town of Cheshire. The city has a long and fascinating history, which dates back to the Roman occupation 2,000 years ago when it was known as Deva, although shards of pottery found at Abbey Green is evidence that there was an earlier settlement here in Neolithic times.

Standing on a strategically important site on a promontory of local red sandstone, Chester grew up on the banks of the lovely River Dee, first as an important Roman military base and harbour, and later flourishing as a trading centre and the largest port in north-west England in the Middle Ages. In the 18th and 19th centuries, the Industrial Revolution brought canals and the railway to the city.

Chester is an exceptionally well-preserved walled city, enclosed by the most complete set of medieval walls in the country. Encircling the city, the two-mile-long walls are a striking reminder of the historic importance of this fortified town and also provide splendid views of the city and the River Dee.

The arrival of the Normans in the 11th century saw the founding of a castle here. Originally a motte-and-bailey fortress, built under the orders of William the Conqueror, Chester Castle later became the frontier base from which North Wales was attacked, and eventually conquered. The oldest remains encompass fragments of the 12th century inner bailey curtain wall, the Flag Tower and the original inner bailey gateway, which are complemented by later additions built in the

Bridge Street

neoclassical style between 1788 and 1813.

Magnificent Chester Cathedral, built like the city walls of local red sandstone, stands on the site of an ancient shrine, which later became the foundations of a Benedictine abbey, before being granted cathedral status in 1541. Much of the Romanesque cathedral was rebuilt in the Gothic style, after much remodelling took place from the 13th to the 16th centuries. In the 14th century, the monks at the Abbey of St. Werburgh first put on the now famous Chester Mystery Plays, which re-created stories from the Bible, a tradition subsequently taken over by the Chester Guilds, but later banned during the Reformation. The plays were revived in 1951 for the Festival of Britain and are today performed every five years.

Chester is particularly famous for its notable black-and-white architecture and 13th century shopping galleries, the picturesque Rows. These are half-timbered buildings of shops, joined by covered galleries and reached by steps from the road. During the 17th and 18th centuries, many of the Rows were enclosed, however, the late 19th century saw the revival of this unique feature as the Victorians brought the two-tiered galleries with their balustraded walkways back in fashion, adding oriel windows and decorative timber-work.

The historic centre of the city follows four main roads, which were first laid out by the Romans, and meet at The Cross by St. Peter's Church. It was here that merchants met in the Middle Ages, when the town flourished as a trading centre, and today, visitors gather here to see the traditional midday proclamations by the flamboyant town criers. This ancient city, where medieval houses mix happily with Tudor and Victorian buildings, exudes a completely unique atmosphere. It is an architectural gem and acknowledged as one of Europe's greatest heritage cities.

The West Front, Chester Cathedral

The Town Hall

Topped by a 160-feet-high tower and spire, Chester's Town Hall was completed in 1869 and stands in Northgate Street in the heart of the city. A magnificent Victorian edifice, the hall was built in Gothic style from banded pink and buff sandstone with a grey-green slate roof. An evocative bronze sculpture entitled 'The Celebration of Chester' was erected in 1992 in front of the Town Hall. Created by the artist, Stephen Broadbent, the three elements of the artwork symbolise Thanksgiving, Protection and Industry.

Westminster Coach & Motor Car Works
This elaborate façade of moulded terracotta bricks, in the Edwardian Baroque style, dates from 1913–14, when the Westminster Coach and Motor Car Works was rebuilt following a fire.

Pied Bull Inn, Lorimer's Row
Believed to have had a licence since 1155, the Pied Bull Inn, part of Lorimer's Row, is an old coaching inn, which is reputedly haunted by the ghost of a cellar man who died here in 1609.

Abbey Square
Handsome Georgian terraced houses, mainly built between 1754 and 1761, line the fine green at Abbey Square. Laid out in the middle of the 18th century, this was originally the site of the old Abbey brewery and bakehouse.

The Abbey Gateway
With elaborate sandstone vaulting dating from the mid-14th century, the Abbey Gateway was built to protect the cathedral precincts. It was also here that gifts were distributed to the poor in medieval times, and where the Chester Mystery Plays were performed.

Addleshaw Tower
A distinctive new bell tower, designed by George Pace, was added to the cathedral in 1975. The first detached bell tower to be built for a cathedral in England since the 15th century, it houses a ring of twelve bells, named after famous saints.

Chester Cathedral
Built of local red sandstone, magnificent Chester Cathedral stands on the site of an ancient shrine. A Benedictine abbey was founded here in the 11th century and flourished for nearly 500 years, before it was granted cathedral status in 1541.

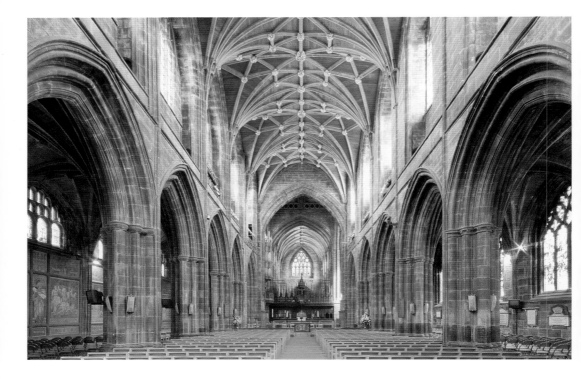

The Nave, Chester Cathedral
The generously proportioned and
magnificent nave of Chester Cathedral is
given a warm and mellow appearance by the
pinkish colour of the sandstone. The south
side of the nave was remodelled in 1360
to change the style from Romanesque to
Gothic, with the north side following
some 130 years later.

St. Werburgh's Shrine, Chester Cathedral
This holy shrine is situated in the Lady
Chapel and adorned with a carving of
St. Werburgh by Joseph Pyrz, added in
1993. The shrine incorporates fragments of
the medieval shrine, which was dismantled
during the Dissolution of the Monasteries.

The Choir, Chester Cathedral
The superb choir, where the monks once held their services, is entered through a screen designed by
Sir George Gilbert Scott and its lectern takes the form of an eagle, symbolising John the Evangelist.
Considered to be the finest in England, the exquisitely carved oak choir stalls date from around 1380
and depict scenes of medieval life, mythological creatures and illustrations of Bible stories.

The Refectory and Cloisters, Chester Cathedral

The Refectory was where the monks once gathered for dinner, and the exquisite stone-canopied pulpit, considered the finest in the country, was used for the reading of the Bible during meal times. Recalling the monastic origins of the cathedral, the fine cloisters date from the early 12th century. Adjoining the Refectory is the North Cloister, which was largely rebuilt during the final days of the abbey.

Eastgate Street

With its pleasing mix of architectural styles, Eastgate Street follows the line of one of the original Roman roads. In the 18th and 19th centuries, it became a fashionable retail centre, and was often compared to London's Regent Street. The Eastgate was erected in 1769 and replaced a large medieval structure, which boasted battlements, turrets and a central tower. The clock, which surmounts the present gateway, was added in 1897 in honour of Queen Victoria's Diamond Jubilee.

Shoemaker's Row

On the west side of Northgate Street stands this beautiful row of shops. Known as Shoemaker's Row, it owes its superb architecture to redevelopment undertaken at the end of the 19th century. Unlike the typical Rows, it has a street-level arcade of shops with the first floor heavily adorned by oriel windows and picturesque gables.

St. Peter's Church

Founded in AD 907 by Ethelfleda of Mercia, St. Peter's is the oldest church in Chester and stands at the heart of the city behind the High Cross where the four main roads meet. Built on the site of the Roman army headquarters, it has an unusual square plan and is the Guild Church of the City.

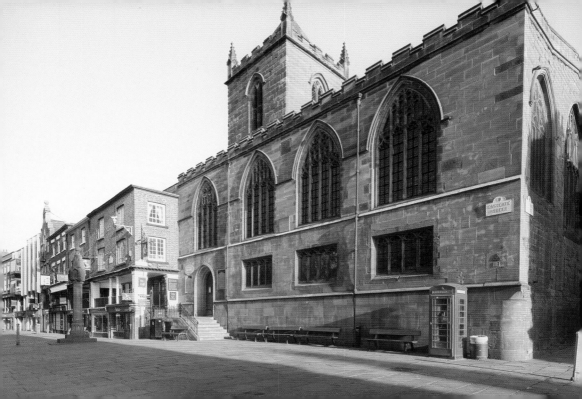

The Cross
The High Cross stands in the centre of Chester at the point where the four Roman roads intersect. It was here that merchants met in the Middle Ages when the city flourished as a trading centre.

Watergate Street Rows
Extending from The Cross to the Watergate, Watergate Street is one of the most beautiful streets in Chester, and it contains some particularly fine examples of the famous Rows.

Bishop Lloyd's Palace

Bishop Lloyd's Palace, in Watergate Street, is one of the finest examples of a half-timbered Tudor house in Chester. Rebuilt in the 17th century when two houses were merged to form one, it has a richly carved frontage, which depicts animals and Biblical scenes.

Stanley Palace

Another of Chester's black-and-white gems, Stanley Palace, in Watergate Street, was built in 1591 for the city's Member of Parliament. In the 19th century this splendid mansion, with its highly decorated façade, was saved from demolition and underwent major restoration.

Bridge Street

Beautiful Bridge Street runs along the line of an old Roman street, the Via Praetoria, and contains some of the best examples of the Chester Rows. The layout of the Rows dates from the 13th century, but there has been constant development over the centuries. Bridge Street Rows give access to a beautiful glass-roofed arcade which, in turn, opens into a modern shopping mall.

Chester Heritage Centre

St. Michael's Church is today home to Chester Heritage Centre, which was the first of its kind to open in Britain. One of nine medieval churches in the city, the church was substantially rebuilt in 1849 and stands on the corner of Bridge Street and Pepper Street.

The Falcon Inn

Home to the Grosvenor family during the Civil War, the Falcon Inn once incorporated part of the Chester Rows, but along with other houses in Lower Bridge Street, it was enclosed in the 17th century. The original 13th century stone piers, which once formed the front of the building, can still be seen inside.

Ye Olde Kings Head

Formerly a town house built in 1208, the picturesque Ye Olde Kings Head in Lower Bridge Street dates from 1622. It contains some notable Elizabethan fireplaces and a timber beam taken from one of Admiral Lord Nelson's ships which sank off the coast of Blackpool.

The Bear and Billet Inn

Built for the Earls of Shrewsbury in 1664, the Bear and Billet Inn, in Lower Bridge Street, is considered to be the finest 17th century timber-framed town house in Chester. The vast mullioned windows are topped by a set of double doors in the gable, giving access to a grain loft, while the frame is made from oak.

The Groves
The pretty Edwardian bandstand is part of the attractive riverside area known as The Groves, and the first concert took place here in 1913. The old Recorder House is one of a row of picturesque 18th century houses which sit in an enviable position high on the southern section of the city walls, looking down over The Groves and the River Dee.

River Dee

Chester was founded at the head of the River Dee estuary, and by the 12th century, it had become one of the most important ports in the country. Today, the river is used for a wide variety of water sports and rowing regattas are often held here. Offering enjoyable riverside walks, The Groves is a delightful promenade which runs from Lower Bridge Street to Grosvenor Park.

Grosvenor Park
Occupying a large tract of land by the River Dee and donated to the city by Richard Grosvenor, the Second Marquess of Westminster, Grosvenor Park has a fine Victorian-style layout with formal avenues and colourful flower beds. Opened to the public in 1867, the park contains three relics from old Chester, which were moved here in Victorian times, including a doorway from St. Michael's Church.

The Roman Amphitheatre
The ruins of this large Roman amphitheatre were first discovered in 1929, and is today the subject of a major archaeological project. It was constructed on a bluff overlooking the River Dee, outside the legionary fortress.

The Hermitage
Also known as the Anchorite's Cell, this unusual little sandstone dwelling has had a varied life, starting out as a religious retreat for monks or hermits in the mid-14th century.

St. John's Priory
Situated near Grosvenor Park overlooking the River Dee, the romantic remains of Chester's first cathedral stand at the eastern end of the present day St. John's Church. Built on the site of an earlier Saxon church, which was founded by King Æthelred of Mercia in about AD 689, the red sandstone ruins encompass the 14th century chancel, the lady chapel and the choir.

The Wishing Steps
Legend has it that anyone who runs up and down the Wishing Steps whilst holding their breath will have their wish come true. The steps were built in 1785 to connect the two levels of walls.

The Roman Garden
Created in 1949, the Roman Garden contains columns and other Roman artefacts which have been found around the city. Today, it provides a tranquil space away from the bustle of the city.

Eastgate Clock

Supported on an ornamental ironwork frame, the beautiful Eastgate Clock was erected in 1897 in celebration of Queen Victoria's Diamond Jubilee. The famous clock was designed by local architect, John Douglas, and the structure is today Grade I listed.

Nine Houses

Only six of the original nine almshouses in Park Street close to the city walls survive today. These delightful small cottages were built around 1650 using a timber-framed structure on a sandstone base and were restored in 1969. Prospective residents had to be over 65 years old and abstain from alcohol and tobacco.

The City Walls

Forming an almost complete circular route around the city centre, Chester's walls provide an enjoyable way to see many of the city's important heritage sights. The earliest surviving section dates back to pre-AD 120 and the most recent was added in 1966.

King Charles Tower

The north-east corner tower of the city walls, King Charles Tower was once known as Newton's Tower and later as Phoenix Tower. The plaque above the door was carved in 1613 and carries the Phoenix symbol of the Painters, Glaziers, Embroiderers and Stationers Company, which used the tower as a meeting place.

LUE COAT HOSPITA[L]

Bluecoat Boy

Added to the school building in the 1850s, the delightful statue of a Bluecoat Boy was modelled on a pupil here, one John Coppack, who was 14 years old at the time. The blue coats signified a boarder, whereas the day scholars where known as Green Caps.

Bluecoat School, Northgate

Originally established by public subscription in 1700, the Blue Coat Hospital was created to educate poor boys. The first charity school outside London, the school dates from 1717 and was built on the site of a medieval hospital. The old school is today part of University College, Chester.

Canal Basin

Chester Canal Basin is set on the Wirral Line of the Shropshire Union Canal, not far from the junction with the Chester Canal and the River Dee at Raymond Street. Once an important junction and distribution centre, Chester is today a popular centre for canal holidays and Tower Wharf is a much-used mooring station. The finest section of the Roman Wall overlooks the canal near Northgate.

Water Tower
Delightful Water Tower Gardens are overlooked by the old Water Tower and Bonewaldesthorne's Tower, which was named after an officer in the army of Ethelfleda in the 10th century.

Goblin Tower
Partly rebuilt after collapsing, the Goblin Tower started life as a completely round tower. It is also known as Pemberton's Parlour, after a local rope maker and former Mayor of Chester.

Chester Races

The oldest racecourse in Britain, Chester Racecourse was created on reclaimed land, known as the Roodee, which once lay under water as a tidal pool of the River Dee. The site of a Roman harbour, the first race took place here during the reign of Henry VIII in 1539.

Grosvenor Museum

This classic 19th century building was designed by Thomas Meakin Lockwood and houses a fascinating museum. Covering over 2,000 years of history, spread over its three floors, the museum was founded in 1885 and is noted for its internationally important collection of Roman stones.

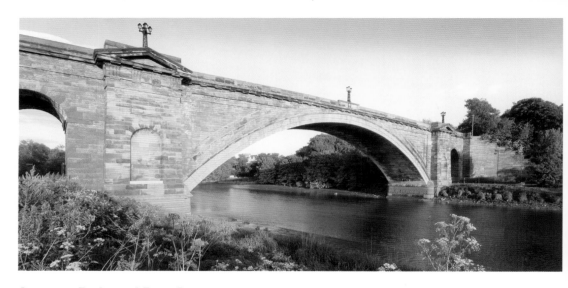

Grosvenor Bridge and River Dee
The 200-feet-span stone arch of Grosvenor Bridge, which was built to help ease congestion on the Old Dee Bridge, was the longest in the world when it was opened in 1832 by the young Princess Victoria. First used by traffic in 1833, it was originally a toll bridge, and before the silting up of the River Dee, it rose to a height of 60 feet allowing the masts of sailing ships to pass underneath.

Chester Castle

Standing on a low hill within a bend of the River Dee, the medieval remains of Chester Castle encompass the three-storey Agricola Tower, which was the original inner bailey gateway and holds the Chapel of St. Mary de Castro as well as some exceptionally fine wall-paintings dating from around 1220. Much rebuilt and extended over the centuries, large parts of the castle complex were built in the neoclassical style, and today house the Crown Court and a military museum.

Published by J. Salmon Ltd., Sevenoaks, Kent TN13 1BB © 2009
Website: www.jsalmon.co.uk Telephone: 01732 452381 Email: enquiries@jsalmon.co.uk
Design and photographs by John Curtis © John Curtis
ISBN 978-1-84640-241-8
Front cover photograph: Eastgate Back cover photograph: Abbey Square
Title page photograph: Chester Art Gallery This page photograph: Old Dee Bridge

Salmon Books

ENGLISH IMAGES SERIES

Photography by John Curtis

Titles available in this series

English Abbeys and Priories

English Gardens

English Country Towns

English Cottages

English Landscape Gardens

English Follies

English Villages

English Country Pubs

English Castles

English Cathedrals

English Country Churches

Jane Austen's England

Romantic England

Mysterious England